AF598971

INFLUENTIAL
WOMEN IN SPACE
GOLRIZ GOLKAR
childsworld.com

Published by The Child's World®
800-599-READ • www.childsworld.com

Photography Credits
Photographs ©: NASA, cover (astronauts), 1 (astronauts), 9, 13, 14, 20; Shutterstock Images, cover (background), 1 (background), 3 (background), 10; Alexander Skowalsky/Noun Project, cover (icon), 1 (icon), 3 (icon), back cover; Roscosmos/Pictorial Press Ltd/Alamy, 5; Nick Ansell/PA Wire/AP Images, 7; Pablo Martinez Monsivais/AP Images, 17; Robert Markowitz/NASA, 19

ISBN Information
9781503889552 (Reinforced Library Binding)
9781503890299 (Portable Document Format)
9781503891531 (Online Multi-user eBook)
9781503892774 (Electronic Publication)

LCCN 2023950314

Printed in the United States of America

Golriz Golkar is the author of more than 100 nonfiction and fiction books for children. She holds a bachelor of arts in American literature and culture from the University of California, Los Angeles, and a master of education in language and literacy from the Harvard Graduate School of Education. Inspired by her work as an elementary school teacher, she loves to write the kinds of books that students are excited to read. Golkar lives in France with her husband and young daughter. She thinks children are the very best teachers, and she loves learning from her daughter every day.

TABLE OF CONTENTS

VALENTINA TERESHKOVA

Valentina Tereshkova was born in the Soviet Union in 1937. She loved parachuting as a young woman. In 1962, the Soviet government decided to send the first female cosmonaut to space. Astronauts from Russia or the Soviet Union are called cosmonauts. Tereshkova and four other women began training. Tereshkova was known for her parachuting skills. She worked hard. She did parachute jumps. She learned how to handle being weightless.

Tereshkova made more than 150 parachute jumps before becoming a cosmonaut.

In 1963, the Soviet government chose Tereshkova to become the first woman in space. She launched on June 16, 1963. She was the only person in her spacecraft. Once in space, she did different tests. The tests helped scientists understand how being in space affects the human body. She also took photos of Earth. These photos helped scientists learn about the **atmosphere**. Tereshkova **orbited** Earth once every 88 minutes. She circled the planet 48 times. She spent almost three days in orbit. Then her spacecraft flew back into Earth's atmosphere. When she was close to Earth, she parachuted back to land.

Tereshkova went to space in the *Vostok 6* spacecraft.

Tereshkova later became an **engineer**. She is still the only woman who has flown alone in space. She paved the way for other female space leaders.

SALLY RIDE

Sally Ride was born in California in 1951. She was a curious child. She loved to play sports and study. As an adult, she almost started a career playing tennis. But she went to college instead. She studied English and physics. Physics is the branch of science that studies how energy and materials interact.

Ride saw an advertisement in the newspaper one day. The National Aeronautics and Space Administration (NASA) wanted to train female astronauts.

Ride's athletic gifts helped her train to be an astronaut.

Ride applied for the job. She was one of six women chosen to train. In 1983, Ride was ready to join a **space shuttle** mission. She became the first American woman in space.

PARTS OF THE SPACE SHUTTLE

The orbiter and the rocket boosters of the space shuttle could be reused for multiple missions.

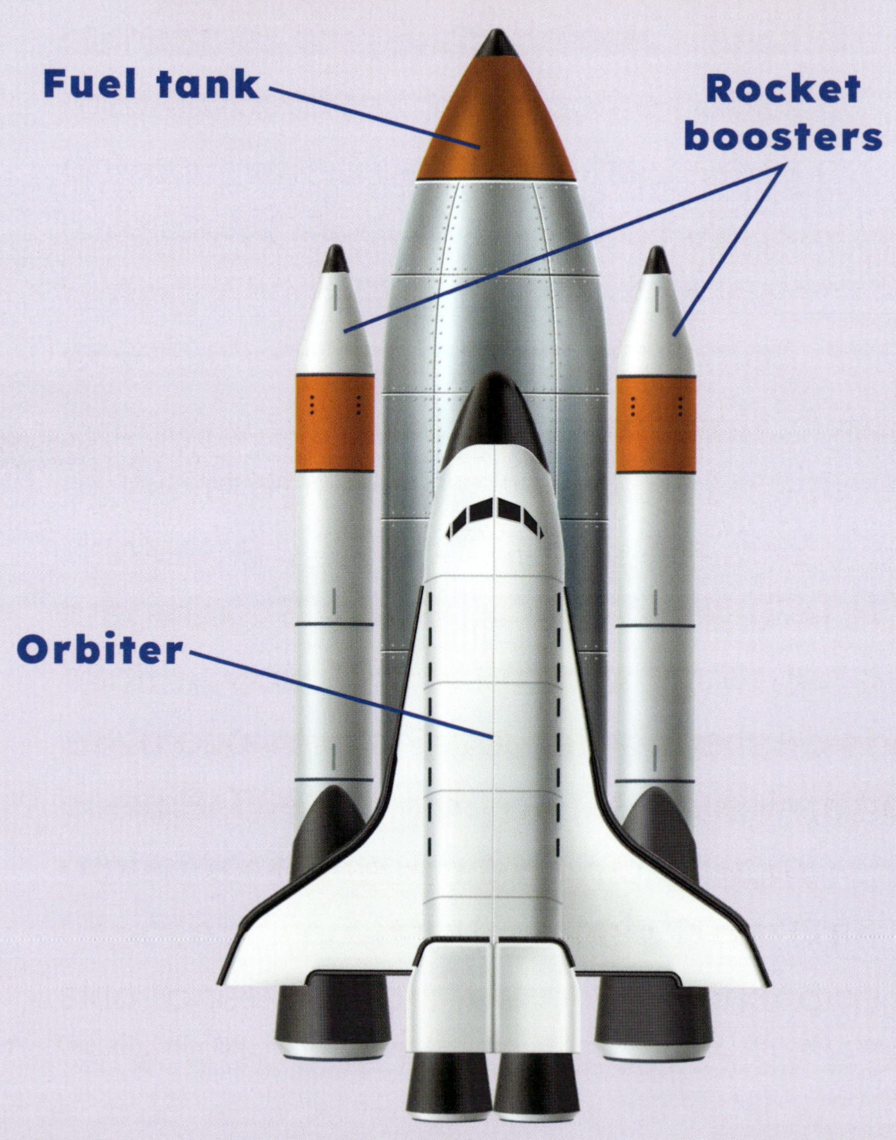

Ride had a special job on the space shuttle. She used a robotic arm to put **satellites** in space. She returned to space a year later on another mission. This time, she used the robotic arm to remove ice from the shuttle. After her space shuttle missions, she helped NASA fix problems with other space shuttles.

Ride left NASA in 1987. She wrote books for children about her adventures. Her books encouraged girls to study science. Ride also helped NASA work with children. She had an idea to place a camera on the **International Space Station** (ISS). Kids could use a computer on Earth to control the camera and take pictures. Ride helped children reach for the stars.

MAE JEMISON

In 1956, Mae Jemison was born in Alabama. She loved science as a child. Jemison watched space missions on TV. She noticed that there were no female astronauts in the United States. This made Jemison sad. But she was inspired by an actress on the TV show *Star Trek*. Her name was Nichelle Nichols. Like Jemison, Nichols was a Black woman. Someday, Jemison dreamed, she would fly to space for real.

Before becoming an astronaut, Jemison worked as a doctor in West Africa for the Peace Corps.

Jemison studied the effect of space travel on bones.

Jemison went to college and became a doctor. But she still wanted to be an astronaut. One day, she learned that Sally Ride was going to space. Jemison was inspired. She applied to NASA in 1987. They accepted her. Jemison began training to become an astronaut.

Jemison went on her first mission in 1992. She was the first Black woman in space. She used her medical training to do tests. Sometimes people get sick on car rides, especially while reading. This is called motion sickness. It can happen in space, too. Jemison looked at the effects of motion sickness in space. She also tested the effects of weightlessness on the body. Jemison even studied how frogs are born in space. She and her crew orbited Earth for eight days.

Jemison was an astronaut for six years. She then taught college classes and opened a scientific research business. She also started a space camp. In 2001, she wrote a children's book about her life. She talked to adults and children about the importance of math and science. Jemison even became the first real astronaut to appear on *Star Trek*. She proved that believing in yourself can make dreams come true.

In 2009, Jemison went to the White House to help students look at stars through telescopes.

EILEEN COLLINS

Eileen Collins began her career in the military. She worked as an instructor and a pilot. NASA then chose her for their astronaut training program. She became the first woman to fly a NASA space shuttle in 1995. She also became the first female commander of a shuttle mission in 1999.

KATE RUBINS

Kathleen (Kate) Rubins dreamed of being an astronaut as a child. She read space magazines. She liked to learn about galaxies. But she also wanted to be a biologist. She wanted to learn about living things. In college, she studied bacteria and viruses.

In 2009, NASA selected a group of people to become astronauts. Rubins was one of them. She flew to the ISS in 2016. She lived there for months with other astronauts. She and her team did more than 200 scientific experiments.

One experiment involved growing heart cells in space. Others were **microbiology** experiments. Rubins also went on spacewalks. A spacewalk is when an astronaut exits a spacecraft while in space. Rubins set up special cameras outside the ISS. They helped people on Earth see what the planet looks like from space.

Jessica Meir waves at the camera during her first spacewalk on October 18, 2019. She and Christina Koch made history that day with the first all-female spacewalk.

Rubins has spent more than 300 days in space. She has done four spacewalks. Her experiments help doctors. They are learning how to treat astronauts who get sick in space. They are also learning about germs that grow on the ISS. Rubins is also helping doctors study the human heart. They are discovering new heart problems and treatments. The doctors want to help astronauts get healthy before going to space.

WONDER MORE

Wondering about New Information

How much did you know about female astronauts before reading this book? What new information did you learn? Write down three new facts that this book taught you. Was the new information surprising? Why or why not?

Wondering How It Matters

What is one way that space science relates to your life? If you cannot think of a personal connection, think about how it might affect other people. What impact could space science have on people's lives?

Wondering Why

Astronauts have to complete lots of training before going on a space mission. Scientists also want to learn how to keep astronauts healthy in space. Why do you think it is important for astronauts to be trained and healthy before going to space?

Ways to Keep Wondering

Sending people to space is hard work. After reading this book, what questions do you have about space travel? What can you do to learn more about it?

FAST FACTS

- Valentina Tereshkova was the first woman in space. She did science experiments on the human body during her mission. She also took photos of Earth. She remains the only woman to have flown alone in space.
- Sally Ride was the first American woman in space. She operated a robotic arm on her missions to fix equipment and put satellites in space.
- Ride later helped NASA plan future missions and fix space shuttle problems. She also helped children take photos with NASA's camera equipment.
- Mae Jemison was the first Black woman in space. She was a doctor who had always wanted to be an astronaut. She did science experiments on her missions.
- Jemison later talked to people about the importance of math and science. She created a space camp for kids.
- Kate Rubins is a microbiologist and an astronaut. She has worked on the ISS.
- Rubins has done many experiments about human health, including studying the human heart. She is helping scientists understand how to keep astronauts healthy.

GLOSSARY

atmosphere (AT-muss-feer) The atmosphere is a big mass of air surrounding Earth. Spacecraft pass through the atmosphere and enter space.

engineer (en-juh-NEER) An engineer is someone who builds or creates machines such as engines. An engineer can help design spacecraft.

International Space Station (in-tur-NASH-uh-nul SPAYS STAY-shun) The International Space Station (ISS) is a large spacecraft that orbits Earth. Some astronauts live on the International Space Station for months at a time.

microbiology (my-kro-by-AH-luh-jee) Microbiology is the study of very small living things. Kate Rubins has done microbiology experiments in space.

orbited (OR-bit-id) Orbited means circled around. The ISS has orbited the Earth since 1998.

satellites (SAT-uh-lites) Satellites are machines or objects that orbit larger objects in space. Some satellites send information about space to scientists back on Earth.

space shuttle (SPAYS SHUH-tul) A space shuttle was a reusable spacecraft that carried people and things to space and back to Earth. Sally Ride rode a space shuttle in 1983.

FIND OUT MORE

In the Library

Alexander, Heather. *Dr. Mae Jemison: Brave Rocketeer*. New York, NY: Harper, 2021.

Ringstad, Arnold. *Space Missions.* Parker, CO: The Child's World, 2021.

Rose, Rachel. *Christina Koch: Astronaut and Engineer*. Minneapolis, MN: Bearport, 2021.

On the Web

Visit our website for links about women in space:
childsworld.com/links

Note to Parents, Caregivers, Teachers, and Librarians: We routinely verify our web links to make sure they are safe and active sites. So encourage your readers to check them out!

INDEX